MAUI
TRAVELOGUE

Text by **CURT SANBURN**
Photography by **DOUGLAS PEEBLES**

MUTUAL PUBLISHING

Once a bustling port of call for the whaling industry of the mid-Pacific, Lahaina harbor is now home to a small fleet of charter fishing boats and pleasure craft. The red-roofed Pioneer Inn is a gentle reminder of those bawdy days of

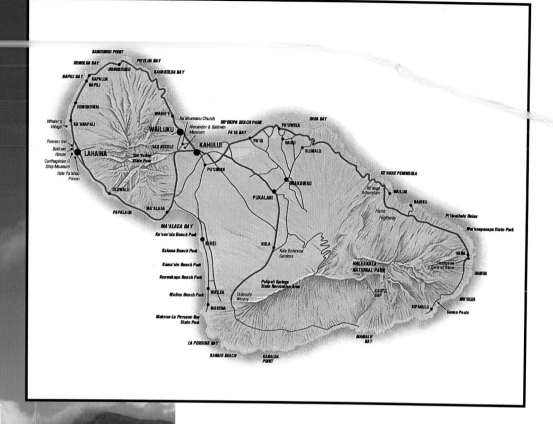

TABLE
OF CONTENTS

FACTS AND FIGURES   5

INTRODUCTION   7

VIGNETTES   11

NATURAL SPECTACLES   15

TOURS   23

BEACHES   47

ADVENTURES   57

CIVILIZATION   63

At Manawainui, along the windward cliffs of Haleakala between Kipahulu and Kaupo, dozens of rain-fed waterfalls carve a series of deep ravines and hanging valleys. Splash pools collect the cascading water and funnel runoff toward the ocean thousands of feet below.

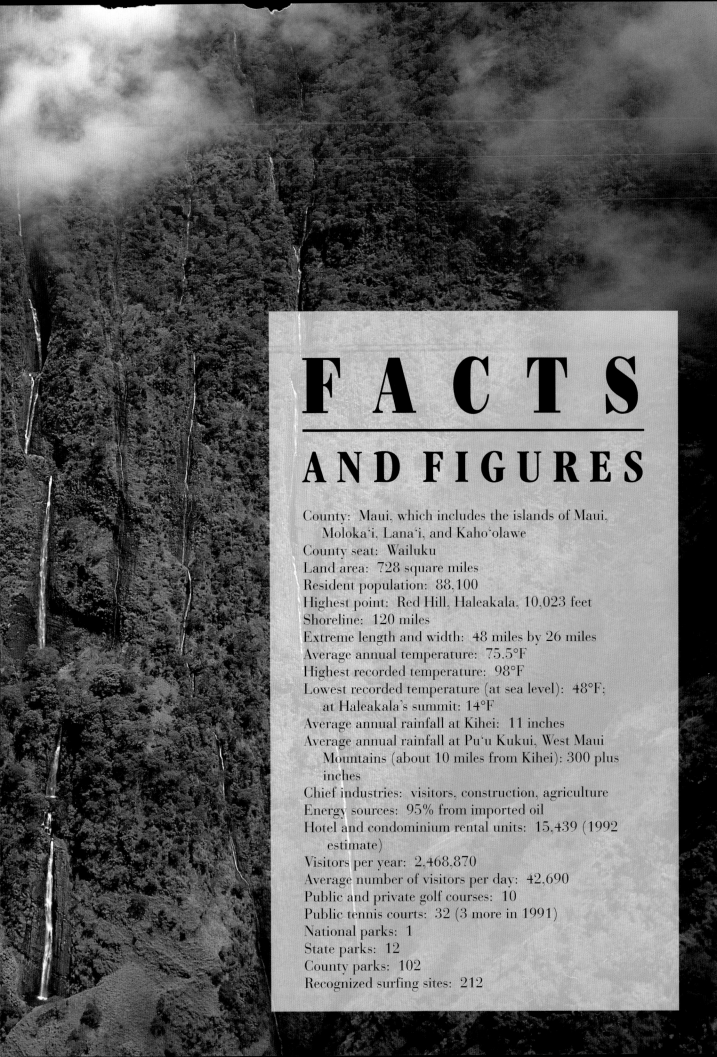

FACTS

AND FIGURES

County: Maui, which includes the islands of Maui, Moloka'i, Lana'i, and Kaho'olawe

County seat: Wailuku

Land area: 728 square miles

Resident population: 88,100

Highest point: Red Hill, Haleakala, 10,023 feet

Shoreline: 120 miles

Extreme length and width: 48 miles by 26 miles

Average annual temperature: 75.5°F

Highest recorded temperature: 98°F

Lowest recorded temperature (at sea level): 48°F; at Haleakala's summit: 14°F

Average annual rainfall at Kihei: 11 inches

Average annual rainfall at Pu'u Kukui, West Maui Mountains (about 10 miles from Kihei): 300 plus inches

Chief industries: visitors, construction, agriculture

Energy sources: 95% from imported oil

Hotel and condominium rental units: 15,439 (1992 estimate)

Visitors per year: 2,468,870

Average number of visitors per day: 42,690

Public and private golf courses: 10

Public tennis courts: 32 (3 more in 1991)

National parks: 1

State parks: 12

County parks: 102

Recognized surfing sites: 212

Although "Ho'okipa" is the Hawaiian word for hospitality, this beach is known for a treacherous rock shelf and strong ocean currents—making it dangerous for swimming, but perfect for windsurfing. Major international windsurfing contests are held here from October to April. Windsurfers catapult into the air, do miraculous flips and spins, land "splat" on the water's surface, and then jibe through the waves again.

INTRODUCTION

The island of Maui gets its name from a mischievous, muscular Polynesian demigod, Maui, who stole the secret of fire from the gods and slowed the sun's flight across the sky so Hawaiian days would be longer and warmer.

Like its namesake, the island of Maui revels in the sun and devotes its long days to playful and athletic pleasures. It is the most glamorous and flamboyant of all the Hawaiian Islands. With miles of swimming beaches, two perpetually sunny coasts, awesome mountains, and calm, leeward seaways ringed by a scenic fleet of lesser islands, Maui has every right to its gilded reputation, its international allure, and the phrase used to describe it: *Maui no ka 'oi,* "Maui is the best!"

Maui, the second youngest and the second largest of Hawai'i's eight major islands, includes in its 728-square-mile landmass two distinct volcanic domes—mighty Haleakala ("House of the Sun") and the compact West Maui Mountains. Haleakala rises 10,023 feet above sea level, while the older West Maui Mountains have a maximum height of 5,778 feet at the top of Pu'u Kukui. The two eroded volcanoes are joined by central Maui's broad, flat isthmus, formed about a million years ago when lava from Haleakala met the shores of West Maui. The isthmus

The crescent-shaped islet of Molokini rises 150 feet out of the waters off Kihei and Ma'alaea. Its sea-breached crater wall harbors a small beach just inside the protective "U" of the collapsed volcano. Legend has it that the island was once a beautiful woman who was turned into stone by Pele, the fire goddess.

functions as a broad valley between the peaks; thus, Maui's nickname, "the Valley Isle."

Offshore are four junior islands, all part of Maui County. Sleepy Moloka'i struggles to maintain its rural character. Lana'i was recently transformed from a pineapple plantation to an exclusive private resort. Kaho'olawe was a U.S. Navy bombing target for many years. And Molokini, a tiny crescent-shaped volcanic cone, is very popular as a snorkeling destination.

Together with the Big Island of Hawai'i, Maui was the stage for ancient Hawai'i's most important events and wars. An era of peace between the rival chiefs of Maui and Hawai'i gave way in the 1600s to two centuries of endless bloodshed. The Maui dynasty of Kekaulike and his son Kahekili was finally defeated in 1790 by the powerful chief from the Big Island, Kamehameha the Conqueror.

By 1802, Kamehameha had unified all the Hawaiian Islands except Kaua'i (which he obtained peacefully in 1810). As the first king of a united Hawai'i, he established his royal capital at Lahaina on Maui's leeward coast.

To show his respect for the superior Maui bloodlines, and to secure those bloodlines for his royal heirs,

Kamehameha married two of Maui's most chiefly women: Ka'ahumanu and the sacred princess Ke'opuolani. After his death, his Maui queens retired the old Hawaiian gods and, at the urging of their Protestant missionary advisors, led the Hawaiian conversion to Christianity. *Heiau*, the simple stone temples of Hawaiian worship, were torn down and replaced by churches and schools, where texts printed in the Hawaiian language taught spiritual and practical learning.

Whales put Maui on the map 150 years ago, when whalers from the eastern U.S. and Europe used the safe and convenient anchorage at Lahaina for a central provisioning stop in the whale-rich northern Pacific. As many as 400 ships dropped anchor there every year during the 1840s. Grog shops and lawlessness proliferated, along with commerce and growth. At the time, Lahaina's native and foreign population was about 3,500 people and 528 dogs.

The discovery of petroleum in Pennsylvania in 1871 put an abrupt end to the whale oil business and the whaling fleets. The royal seat of the kingdom was moved to the larger commercial port at Honolulu on O'ahu. Lahaina was all but deserted.

For the next century, Maui slumbered as its vast lands were consolidated into sugar cane and pineapple plantations, and its mountain streams were tapped for irrigation water. Until the early 1960s, Maui was little more than a few plantation camps, cattle ranches, isolated fishing villages, a half-dozen Spartan hotels, and plenty of space. The sugar fields spread uninterrupted like rich lawns from the foot of the mountains to the beaches.

Sliced into the lush green coast of east Maui, the winding road to the remote paradise of Hana town is famous for its dangerously narrow hairpin turns, waterfall-misted gully bridges, stands of giant bamboo, fern grottoes, and sparsely populated valleys.

The tourist boom began at Ka'anapali in 1962. For the next 25 years and continuing today, resort hotels, golf courses, and vacation condominiums have seemed to sprout wherever there is a sunny swimming beach. Little Kahului airport, long accustomed to a few inter-island flights daily, found itself welcoming nonstop jumbo jets direct from mainland U.S. cities.

At the same time, mainland hippies found the deeper meaning of "mellow" on Maui's remote beaches and in the smoky haze of its famous *pakalolo* (marijuana). The island became a world-renowned playground for the Age of Aquarius.

The current Maui lifestyle now attracts large numbers of "life-stylists" to the island's seaside condominiums and chic Upcountry cabins. These folk settle down for a few years as realtors, hotel bartenders, carpenters, small shop owners, and trust-fund windsurfers. As a result, Maui is the fastest growing and most heavily *haole* (Caucasian) of all the islands.

About 2-1/2 million visitors now spend $1.5 billion on Maui each year. On an average day, 42,000 visitors share the island with a resident population that has passed the 100,000 mark. Locals grumble about traffic that most newcomers barely notice.

Amid all the glitzy resorts and swank restaurants, Maui manages to keep its island character and its soaring beauty alive. To be enjoyed are its natural and man-made wonders, its country roads, ancient temples, peaceful beaches, blazing sunsets, misty rains, friendly smiles, and dewy flowers.

La Perouse Bay on the southernmost tip of Maui, just below
the 'Ulupalakua Ranch, lies well past civilization. Stunning
cobalt blue water contrasts with the stark black of
Haleakala's most recent lava flow (dated around 1790). The
French explorer La Perouse reported a shallow bay in this
area in 1796. It was mapped and named by Captain George
Vancouver a few years later. From this aerial angle, the
West Maui Mountains loom as an apparition in the distant

M A U I
V I G N E T T E S

EARLY REPORTS FROM THE EXPLORERS

"About a hundred and twenty persons, men and women, waited for us on the shore.... The women showed by the most expressive gestures that there was no mark of kindness they were not disposed to confer upon us, and the men in the most respectful attitude endeavored to discover the motive of our visit in order to anticipate our desires.... I had no idea of a people so mild and attentive."

—from the journal of French navigator Jean Francois Galaup, Comte de la Perouse, who on May 30, 1786 made the first European landing on Maui at Keone'oi'o, now known as La Perouse Bay.

"...They have coarse features, thick eyebrows, black eyes which without being hard express self-confidence, prominent cheekbones, slightly widened nostrils, thick lips, a large mouth, and teeth which are somewhat wide but quite fine and straight. Their hair is black and cut in the pattern of a helmet. Worn very long, like the flowing crest of a helmet, their hair is a reddish brown color at the ends.... These people paint and tattoo their skin. They pierce their ears and nasal septa, and adorn themselves with rings inserted in these parts.

"The inhabitants in general however are mild and engaging in their behavior, and even show toward strangers a degree of politeness.... The dress of both sexes consists of a sort of apron covering what nature bids them conceal, and another piece of similar cloth wrapped around the body."

—from the journal of Dr. Rollin, physician aboard La Perouse's flagship Boussole.

THE SUGAR PLANTATIONS

Brought as a food plant by the Polynesians, sugar cane, a giant grass, was first grown in the Islands commercially in 1802. The enterprise failed. Forty years later, when the California Gold Rush and the American Civil War spurred demand for sugar, large plantations were established here, often on former chiefly and royal lands. A reciprocity treaty with the U.S. reduced import duties on Hawaiian sugar, and by 1890 Hawai'i was exporting 250 million pounds of sugar a year.

Labor was a problem; Hawaiians, ravaged by disease and culture shock, were unable to adapt to plantation life. The plantation owners looked to the Portuguese islands of Madiera and the Azores, then to China, Japan, Korea, and the Philippines for workers. Between 1852 and 1948, roughly 300,000 contract laborers arrived to work the 27 plantations spread across Hawai'i's arable land. When their contracts were up, most of them stayed. The plantations have dwindled, but the descendants of the workers have flourished.

Today the old plantation camps are historically akin to New York's Ellis Island—the place where poor and often frightened people had their first taste of life in a strange and wonderful new land.

THE SPECTACULAR PROTEA—UPCOUNTRY'S MOST EXOTIC EXPORT

Upcountry Maui's rich, well-drained volcanic soil, its warm days and cool nights, and its mix of rain and sun create perfect growing conditions for an amazing family of ancient flowering plants called protea (*pro-tee-uh*). With multilayer, multitexture, and multicolor blossoms, proteas surely rank among the plant world's most elaborate demonstrations of nature's art.

The extraordinarily diverse protea family (more than 1,500 species and varieties have been catalogued) derives its name from the Greek sea god. Proteus, who was able to transform himself into any form he desired. Proteas grow wild in their native South Africa and Australia. The outrageous blossoms created a sensation when European adventurers brought them to the attention of French and British botanists in the eighteenth century. Both England's King George III and Napoleon's Empress Josephine took up hothouse protea cultivation as a hobby.

The flowers were brought to Maui in the early 1960s by pioneering University of Hawai'i botanist David Williams. He planted 50 species on the Kula slopes of Haleakala. An almost immediate commercial success, the durable, colorful blossoms command high prices both locally and in mainland U.S. markets, bringing international recognition to Hawai'i's flower industry.

Roughly 50 species of protea and related banksia grow in Upcountry flower farms. Their colorful names suggest the blossoms' spectacular possibilities: the giant king protea, the giant woolly-beard, woolly-headed protea, the rose-spoon protea, the pink mink, the ermine tail, the candlelite, the Hawaiian sunburst pincushion, the red swamp banksia, the pink star, the silver tree, the flametip, the safari sunset, the woolly banksia, the golden acorn, the raspberry frost, the orange frost.

The gently rolling fence-lined rural roads of Upcountry Maui have the appearance of middle America, except for the dramatic ocean views offered at every turn.

Pink minks and yellow minks hang upside down at a protea farm in Kula.

A pair of Hawaiian pincushion protea lift their filamentous heads to catch the sun. Each of the thin spikes is an individual flower.

A golden banksia glows in the morning light.

Backlit by sunrise, a cloud bank plumes over the West Maui mountains. The southeastern spur of Haleakala in the distance is the site of the last lava flows on the island.

The desolate interior of Haleakala crater has been compared to the surface of the moon. This view from near the visitors' center faces northeast toward the Ko'olau Gap and its near-constant cloud pocket. On the left rise the jagged spires of the Leleiwi cliffs, and on the right the Kalapawili Ridge and its highest point, Hanakauhi peak.

Chill out, Hawaiian style.

Hawaiian Airlines and Hilo Hattie have teamed up to give you a cool deal! When you spend $40 or more at Hilo Hattie, you'll get an exclusive Hawaiian Airlines collapsible 12-pack insulated beverage cooler for free.

世界最大のハワイアンストアー "ヒロ・ハッティ" では、100%品質保証付きの商品が、毎日お得な価格でお求めいただけます。

ヒロ・ハッティで$40以上お買い物をすると、ハワイアン・エアライン特製の折りたたみ式クーラーバッグを差し上げます！JCBをはじめとする各種クレジットカード及び日本円もご使用いただけます。無料送迎サービスもあり。お問い合わせは、日本語ライン 535-6500まで。

Bring in this coupon for your FREE
Hawaiian Airlines Cooler
with purchase of $40 or more at Hilo Hattie.

The Store of Hawaii

Good at Hilo Hattie stores on Oahu, Kauai, Maui, Kona, Hilo, and Orange & San Diego, California. Valid at time of purchase. Coupon must be presented to Hilo Hattie cashier in order to receive the free Hawaiian Airlines Cooler. One cooler per person, per day. While supplies last. Cannot be combined with other offers or coupons. No cash value. Offer expires September 7, 2005.

7 60840 03500 5

Hilo Hattie ~ The Store of Hawaii

Discover Hawaii's largest selection of Hawaiian Fashions, gifts, crafts, souvenirs, t-shirts, home accessories, beauty products and stunning Island jewelry. Hilo Hattie is also the world's largest manufacturer of Hawaiian, resort and casual fashions, offering hundreds of exclusive prints and styles not found in any other store. You'll enjoy our great values and 100% quality guarantee on thousands of Hawaiian products.

Free transportation is available from Waikiki and most outer island hotels.

Hilo Hattie Locations

Honolulu, O'ahu
(Our Flagship Factory Store)
（フラッグシップ・ファクトリーストア）
700 N. Nimitz Highway
Phone: 808-535-6500

Ala Moana Shopping Center
(Street level, ocean side next to McDonald's)
アラモアナショッピングセンター
（ストリートレベル海側、マクドナルド隣り）
Phone: 808-973-3266

Lahaina, Maui
Phone: 808-667-7911

Kihei, Maui
Phone: 808-875-4545

Lihue, Kaua'i
Phone: 808-245-3404

Hilo, Big Island
Phone: 808-961-3077

Kona, Big Island
Phone: 808-329-7200

Orange, California
The Block at Orange
Phone: 714-769-3255

San Diego, California
Gaslamp Quarter
Phone: 619-546-7289

The Store of Hawaii

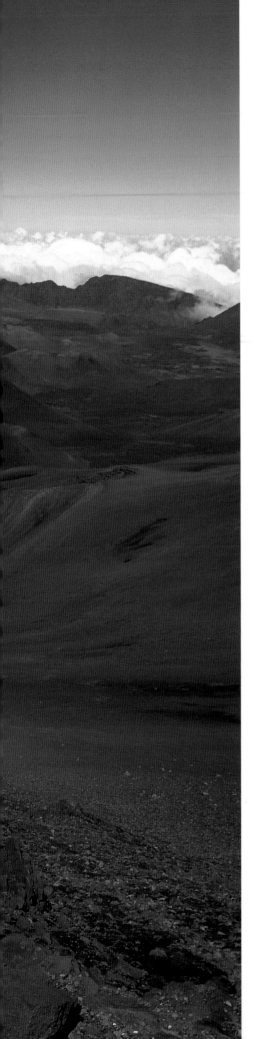

NATURAL
SPECTACLES

Mythology notwithstanding, the 1,600-mile-long chain of the Hawaiian Islands was built by volcanic action beginning roughly 30 million years ago at Kure Atoll, at the north-western end of the archipelago, and continuing today on and near the Big Island at the southeastern end of the chain. A slow, steady north-western drift of the earth's upper layer over a deeper "hot spot" accounts for the island chain's linear shape and the progressive age of the islands within the chain.

The typical landform is the broadly rounded "shield" volcano, built up from the ocean floor to heights in excess of two miles above sea level by innumerable thin lava flows. Mauna Loa on the Big Island is a classic—and still active—shield volcano, so gentle in its rise that its 13,600-foot height (as high as most Rocky Mountain peaks) is difficult to appreciate.

On the eight major islands, it's easy to see the geological evolution from the broad, swelling shapes of young and virtually intact shield volcanoes on the Big Island to the heavily eroded, jagged topography of Kaua'i. Low-lying Ni'ihau island is the almost completely worn-down remains of an even older shield volcano.

On Maui, the dominating mass of dormant Haleakala clearly shows the broad shape of a "young" shield volcano (active as recently as 200 years ago). By contrast, the originally compact West Maui volcano is so deeply dissected that it is now referred to as the West Maui "Mountains." The separate "peaks" are actually the surviving shoulders of the volcano, cut by deeply eroded canyons. Viewed from Makena, however, the West Maui landmass can be seen to retain its overall shield-volcano shape.

The effects of rainfall and resulting stream erosion are most striking on the windward (northeastern) sides of all the islands. Windward Haleakala and West Maui, particularly at 'Iao Valley, show heavy stream erosion. Leeward slopes, where much less rain falls, show relatively little.

Trade wind-driven waves have carved low sea cliffs all along Maui's exposed northeastern coastline. On nearby Moloka'i, the same waves have carved cliffs higher than 2,000 feet, among the highest in the world, on the north shore of the island.

15

The Keʻanae peninsula on the Hana coast is famous for its production of taro. Here a small *loʻi* or taro terrace is nestled near the rugged coast on this heavily vegetated spit of land.

A silversword *keiki* (seedling), like a spiky ball of dull platinum, glistens against the rugged volcanic terrain of Haleakalā.

Puʻu ʻOlaʻi ("red hill") cinder cone, on a jutting piece of land separating the south Maui coast from the back side of Haleakala, is flanked by Makena's Little Beach and Big Beach (Oneloa). This undeveloped area, once zoned for resorts, was acquired for a state park in the late 1980s after a 15-year fight.

Going south past Hana, near the end of the paved road, are the Seven Pools. This natural succession of small waterfalls tumbling into base pools continues in a constant flow to the ocean. The popular swimming holes are a refreshing stop after the long and sometimes torturous drive down the Hana Road. The ancient people named these pools ʻOheʻo, and placed a *kapu* on them that prohibited menstruating women from bathing in the tranquil waters.

Rapid changes in altitude affect your breathing, as you wind
your way into the middle of a vast, desolate, cone-blistered
cup lined with volcanic rust-colored cinder devoid of
vegetation or life.

TOURS

HALEAKALĀ'S UPCOUNTRY

Generations of Upcountry *paniolo* proudly carry on traditions introduced to Hawai'i by Mexican vaqueros. These "espaniol" were brought to the Islands in 1803 to help round up feral horses and cattle.

Crater Road zigzags through Maui's "cloud country" toward the 10,023-foot summit of Haleakalā ("House of the Sun").

Either a morning drive up the volcano, with lunch in Kula on the way down, or a full day's outing to take in all of the mountain's top-to-bottom wonders is a must. While the all-day drive is a strenuous one, it offers everything of interest—including a long, but unforgettable, drive to the spectacular "Dismal Coast" on Haleakalā's south flank. Get an early start.

The drive up through the clouds and the view from the top of Haleakala are among the best reasons to visit Maui. Starting in Kahului, the Route 37, Haleakalā Highway (377), and Crater Road (378) climb past sugar cane fields, emerald truck farms, ranchlands, mist-wrapped stands of eucalyptus and fir, high grasslands, and, above the 7,000-foot cloud line, the alpine shrublands and lava deserts of the summit. Overall, the 38-mile, 90-minute drive climbs two vertical miles, one of the shortest and fastest high-mountain climbs on earth.

At 6,800 feet is the entrance to Haleakalā National Park, which requires a modest entrance fee. Proceed to the Visitor Center perched above Haleakalā valley, where a truly awesome landscape of cinder slopes and multicolor volcanic cones floats above a sea of clouds. Off to the southeast, the volcanic peaks of the Big Island rise. Far below and to the west are the islands of Kaho'olawe, Lana'i, and Moloka'i; on very clear days, even O'ahu can be seen. Self-guided walks along the crater rim, hikes into the crater, as well as guided overnight hikes and horseback trips, are possible (*see* Adventures). It is important, however, to have proper shoes or boots and rain gear, as the weather can change abruptly for the worst, particularly in the crater. (For weather information, contact the park headquarters at the visitor center.)

Watching the sun rise from the summit of Haleakalā is an almost mystical experience. However, get on the road not later than 4 a.m. (5 a.m. during winter months) for the two-hour drive, to arrive at the top in time for the pre-sunrise aurora and subsequent light show. DRESS WARMLY. Wear long pants and take a sweater or jacket—even a hotel blanket.

After the spectacle of sunrise has passed and the light is strong, visit the park headquarters just inside the park entrance to learn the lore of Haleakalā and to catch a glimpse of the state bird of Hawai'i, the endangered *nene*. The unique and wonderful silversword plant is most easily seen in the vicinity of the Kalahaku overlook turnoff, two miles below the Haleakalā Visitor Center.

Kula Highway and Route 377 follow the 2,000-foot elevation around Haleakalā's western slope through the Kula and 'Ulupalakua countryside. These roads are Upcountry's garden boulevards, where scores of small carnation, chrysanthemum, protea, Kula onion, and lettuce farms create a deeply colored patchwork. Pastures, stands of eucalyptus, and open grasslands spread out beyond the irrigated plots to frame a panorama of the ocean and the rest of Maui lying far below. As if all this were not enough, from April to June the green fields and roadsides are brushed with the luminous lavender flowers of jacaranda trees.

Upcountry has become an important nursery center for exotic plants and flowers. The Sunrise Protea Farm at the bottom of Crater Road (378) near its intersection with Route 377 is a good spot to see cultivated protea. The cut flowers can be mailed anywhere in the United States as gifts.

Two other spots for viewing Maui's exotic flora are the Kula Botanical Gardens on Route 377 two miles south of Route 378, and the University of Hawai'i's Kula Experimental Station on Copp Road, off the Kula Highway.

Beyond the 'Ulupalakua cattle ranch around the southwestern shoulder of Haleakalā, Kula Highway becomes Pi'ilani Highway (31). Near 'Ulupalakua ranch headquarters, among green pastures and groves of eucalyptus, is Tedeschi Vineyards, the only commercial winery on Maui. Wine tastings, offering a Hawaiian *Blanc de Noir*, a "Maui Blush," or a novelty pineapple wine, are held in an old jailhouse near the highway. The winery is open from 9 a.m. to 5 p.m.

Narrow, bumpy Pi'ilani Highway skitters around Haleakalā's southwest volcanic rift zone, well above the beach resorts at Wailea and Mākena, into a prehistoric landscape—what French explorer La Perouse called the "Dismal Coast" when he first saw it in 1786. Haleakalā's vast dry southern flank sweeps relentlessly from the two-mile-high summit to an empty, gale-lashed coast. One or

two ranches, barely noticeable in the vastness, share the sparse grazing. Cattle wander carelessly on the road. Across stormy 'Alenuihaha Channel, the rounded volcanoes of the Big Island, 80 miles south, hang in the sky.

Despite its story-book nickname, the Dismal Coast was home to thousands of Hawaiians when the first westerners arrived. Fishing settlements dotted the rocky coast, and villages growing sweet potatoes and taro spread their lava-rock foundations across upland meadows. Freshwater springs determined the location of these settlements.

Extensive stone terraces, the remains of the village of Kahikinui ("Great Tahiti"), command a plateau a thousand feet above the sea. From Manawainui Gulch, where the Pi'ilani Highway finally descends to sea level, an ancient shoreline trail marked by lines of stones crosses the barrenness all the way to La Perouse Bay. Three miles beyond Manawainui, at Nu'u Bay, thickets hide the symmetrical rock piles and petroglyphs of a long-abandoned fishing village and its canoe launching site.

Hundreds of former house sites (little more than rock piles now) line the coast. Because there has been very little disruption here, the haunting sense of being close to the past is strong along the Dismal Coast. Is that just a rockpile, or a sign of former human life? Who arranged these stones? What joys and sadnesses were lived out on these awesome shores? What gods were conjured to match the harsh grandeur of this land and sea?

From Nu'u Beach, the road climbs a promontory capped by the stone platform of an ancient *heiau*. Less than a mile beyond Nu'u, a broad, flat lava peninsula, Lapehu Point, juts into the surf below. On the windswept point can be seen several symmetrical stone formations, the remains of a fishing shrine. If you still have the energy, and enough daylight remains, the half-hour hike down to the point is a fitting end to your Haleakalā tour. In visiting the site, remember to be respectful in all ways.

Two miles beyond Nu'u Bay, the road becomes impassable, and you must turn around for the long drive back to the twentieth century.

It is said that when the first Spanish-speaking visitors saw this piece of land on the side of Haleakalā, they exclaimed, "O Linda Vista" (oh, beautiful view). Olinda, a classic storybook hamlet of pastures and farms, is nestled just south of the scenic meadows of Haleakalā Dairy and Haleakalā Ranch. Stands of eucalyptus trees lace through the green pastures of this Upcountry community.

Kula, a small community located in Upcountry Maui on the northern slope of Haleakalā, is the farming belt of the island.

Horses, introduced to the Islands by traders seeking royal favor, multiplied in the wild uplands of the Big Island and Maui.

Built in 1897 by Portuguese laborers, the octagonal building of the Holy Ghost Hall of Our Lady Queen of Angels Church stands alone past the small town of Kula, near Waiakoa.

The Erdman-Tedeschi Vineyards, nestled among majestic stands of euculyptus, produces the only commercial wine in the Islands.

The silversword grows up to 50 years before blooming once and dying.

La Perouse Bay, named by Captain George Vancouver in honor of French explorer La Perouse. A dramatic view of nature's contrasts—the glistening, shallow bay embraced by hardened lava which last flowed from Haleakalā around 1790—is captured in this bird's-eye view.

On a tiny surf-pounded peninsula below the Kaupo Ranch is the lonely white coral building of Huialoha (a "Gathering of Love") Church. Commonly known as the Kaupo Church, this old Congregational meeting house was originally built in 1859, a time when Kaupo was almost totally landlocked, accessible only by sea and a primitive trail. An unlocked gate at the road leading to the church welcomes all to visit the grounds.

The cinder cone cluster of Puʻu o Maui ("hill of Maui"), Halaliʻi (named for an Oʻahu trickster demigod), Puʻu Naue ("earthquake hill") stands within the center of Haleakalā.

Selling everything from pre-packaged ti-leaf cuttings to mango chutney, tiny specialty shops, like the Sunrise Protea Store in Upcountry, cater to the rent-a-car tourists that brave the winding roads of Haleakalā's slopes.

Horses graze in the high pastures of ʻUlupalakua Ranch.

The Hana Coast is renowned for its excellent fishing grounds. The land, poured out in layers from numerous eruptions of Haleakala, plunges steeply to great depths, creating the dramatic contrast of verdant cliffs, jet lava, and lapis-blue water. The hazards of fishing and diving in these areas due to sudden high surf and shifting currents have taken many lives, but have not slowed the harvest of the ocean's bounty.

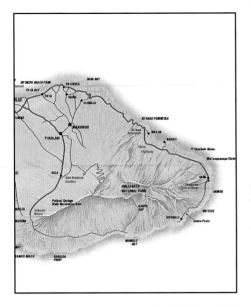

HANA & THE SOUTHEAST COAST

A vaulted tunnel of shower trees and bougainvillea.

The dancers of Haku Mele O Hana perform the *kahiko* (ancient) hula at the Hana Maui Hotel.

This roadside display of country merchandising offers a vivid look into Maui's rural culture.

Set aside a full day for exploring the Hana Coast. Take a swimsuit and towel, mud shoes, and an umbrella or rain coat—just in case—as this is the wettest coast of Maui. For more information on the Hana Coast see *Maui's Hana Highway: A Visitor's Guide* by Angela Kay Kepler (Mutual Publishing).

The two-hour drive (minimum) to Hana from Kahului follows a notoriously winding, narrow road. Traffic bound for Hana peaks at midmorning; the return rush is between 4 and 6 p.m. The trip, as spectacular as it is, can be exhausting.

An alternative schedule to beat the traffic is to begin your trip at midday, eat dinner in Hana, and return in the evening. Driving the Hana Highway at night is not that bad. For most of its length, the road is well marked with reflectors and stripes; headlights of oncoming cars can be seen for hundreds of yards in the darkness. Another possibility, and by far the most relaxed way, is to make advance reservations and spend the night in Hana at the Heavenly Hana Inn, Hana Bay Vacation Rentals, Hana Kai Condominiums, or at any of Hana's handful of small motels or vacation rentals. Driving can then be spread over two days, allowing quality time for exploring the scenic and historic corners of Maui's Garden of Eden.

The tour starts at lower Pa'ia Town on the Hana Highway. Pa'ia, an old plantation "camp," was once a major population center until the master-planned suburbs of Kahului attracted most of its workers away after World War II. The town reawakened in the late 1960s to a gentle invasion of hippies, artists, and other free spirits who spruced up its fading storefronts and added an artsy-craftsy, tofu-and-sprouts overlay. Today colorful Pa'ia is an international meeting place for windsurfers who tackle the big waves and steady winds nearby.

A good place for breakfast, Pa'ia is also the last chance until Hana to fill your gas tank. Then buckle your seat belt and get set for the narrow, 52-mile Hana Highway. Untainted landscapes around every curve (more than 600 of them), waterfalls by the score, 56 bridges, and overwhelmingly rich tropical vegetation are the special pleasures. Watch the mile markers to locate several of the sights described here.

Another thing: Commuting over the tortuous Hana Highway is a daily ordeal for local residents. Please *kokua* (cooperate) and pull over quickly when someone wants to pass.

Baldwin Beach Park, just west of Pa'ia, and Ho'okipa Beach Park (*see* Beaches), just east of the town, are two popular beaches on the Hana Highway with wonderful views across the water to the West Maui Mountains. Baldwin is a local favorite, while Ho'okipa is a world-famous windsurfing spot known for high-performance wave riding, especially in winter months. Spectators have a good view from the parking area above the bay, but the water is not recommended for inexperienced swimmers, except in the shallow pools right at beachside.

Beyond the settlements of Ha'iku and Huelo, the road climbs and twists above the sea cliffs, gulches, and bays to Kailua's neatly tended gardens, and the small dams and ditches of the East Maui Irrigation (EMI) system. By that time, the sugar cane, pineapple, and pasturelands of agricultural Maui have given way to the mostly introduced species of Maui's windward lowland forests. Ironwoods, Norfolk Island pines, *kukui*, guava, mountain apple, African tulip, and *hau* shelter an understory of ferns, gingers, heliconias, and allamanda. Fabulously fragrant white, yellow, and *kahili* ginger blossoms are worth picking if you see their delicate, stringy flower clusters set amid thick green banks of paddle-shape leaves on long stalks. A handful of ginger on your car dashboard will pump out its sweet scent all day.

Crashing surf and bare lava outline the Ke'anae peninsula. It is said that the god Kane thrust his spear into a rock and a fresh-water spring gushed from the hole. Once the site of many fishponds, the peninsula remains a community of taro farmers.

For eating, lemon-size yellow-to-pink guava fruit is conspicuously abundant on roadside bushes. Though seedy, the sweet, mild fruit can be eaten like an apple, skin and all. Small, red-to-pink mountain apples, which ripen in late summer and early fall, are juicy with a pearlike taste. Unfortunately, they tend to hang just out of reach.

A forest canopy of bunchy, soft-green treetops rippling in the wind introduces the Waikamoi region's bamboo forests. At ground level, bamboo stands are dark, impenetrable, and tightly spaced, often broken by the ghostly diagonal lines of fallen stalks. The wind rustles the leafy tops, but inside the grove all is silent. It's no wonder Buddha is said to have loved bamboo forests.

An excellent place to get personal with a tropical forest is the Waikamoi Ridge Trail, one-half mile beyond mile marker 9. The turnout and trail are well marked. On the trail, look for solid, deep red, tightly petalled blossoms about the size of a child's fist. These are 'awapuhi, or "shampoo ginger." Squeeze the smooth, shiny blossom and a thick, sticky liquid, used by Hawaiians as a shampoo/hair conditioner, appears. A national line of expensive hair-care products now uses 'awapuhi in its formulations, so you may as well give it a try. Apply the unscented gook to wet hair, comb through, then rinse. One blossom is enough for a head of hair.

The scenery, particularly the waterfalls, begins to intensify beyond Waikamoi. At Puohokamoa Stream, a pullout (probably with a few cars parked) marks a double waterfall, as well as a swimming pond, reachable by a short trail. (Note: Do not drink free-flowing water anywhere on this coast. Wild upland pigs have brought dangerous bacteria into the watershed.)

You are halfway to Hana when you reach Kaumahina State Wayside Park, where there are beautiful views of Honomanu Bay and Ke'anae peninsula, a short nature trail, picnic tables, drinkable water, and restroom facilities.

Look for the *hala* trees here and all along the rest of your drive, recognizable by their tropical, prehistoric look. Smooth-skinned, patterned limbs rise from exposed bunches of stilt roots to support a canopy of thick, spiralling tufts of shiny, spine-edged leaves. These lovely, romantic trees once covered huge windward areas of all the islands and were essential to the Hawaiians as sources of building materials, medicines, matting, and fishing supplies. Durable *lauhala* mats, made from the stripped, softened, and plaited leaves, were used everywhere until World War II. Unfortunately, the craft of *lauhala* weaving is disappearing.

As you approach the Ke'anae peninsula, at a sharp hairpin turn, the Ke'anae Arboretum is clearly marked on the *mauka* (mountain) side of the road. Maintained by the Hawai'i State Department of Land and Natural Resources, this free facility has a highly informative presentation of Hawai'i's native plants, introduced plants, traditional Hawaiian foodstuff, and material source plants.

Maui's sparkling waterfalls cascade from mountain streams into lava-dark pools typically ringed with fern and ti.

Rainbow shave ice served up at Tutu's snack shop in Hana is a welcome treat after the long drive down the Hana Highway.

Within earshot of the grinding surf along the ragged edge of leaf-shaped Ke'anae peninsula sits one of the earliest of the circuit Congregational churches built around Maui. Erected in 1856, this chapel survived the 1946 tidal wave that claimed the lives of several of its church members.

Beyond the bucolic Keʻanae peninsula, home to a small, private community of Hawaiian taro growers (whose fields are best viewed from an overlook near mile marker 17), there is a rapid succession of waterfalls. Fruit stands sell bananas, papayas, coconuts, mountain apples (in season) and star fruit. Puaʻa Kaʻa State Park, just beyond tiny Wailua, is a good stopping point. The highway then climbs to 1,200 feet, the highest elevation on the road.

The final "must" stop before Hana is the 120-acre Waiʻanapanapa State Park, just beyond the Hana Airport. This popular park offers camping and cabins (permits and reservations needed), a dramatic black-sand beach set in a jagged lava cove, and a series of freshwater caves, reachable by a well-marked trail from the upper parking lot. When the water is calm, snorkeling is excellent. Remnants of the old *alaloa*, long trail, that once circled Maui is found near the caretaker's house and can be followed on foot along the sea cliffs, or all the way into Hana town.

Ancient stone walls, marking Polynesian house sites, *heiau*, and gravesites abound here and should be treated with care. Throughout Hawaiʻi, it is traditional to wrap a small stone in a *ti* leaf and leave it in the forest or directly on old stone walls to show respect for the spirit of a place. Offerings left by others should not be disturbed.

One of Hawaiʻi's loveliest and most remote outposts, the historic garden community of Hana is a relaxing luncheon stop after the dizzying drive. Visit the friendly (and tiny) Hana Cultural Center (Hale O Waiwai O Hana) and the beachfront at Hana Bay for good swimming, views of legendary Kaʻuiki Hill, and the spot in the middle of the bay where Hawaiians have surfed for centuries.

To the right of the pier a short but difficult path leads out to Kaʻuiki Head and the lighthouse beyond. The path passes the birth cave of Hawaiʻi's most historically influential female *aliʻi*, Kaʻahumanu, the favorite wife of King Kamehameha. She encouraged the abandonment of the ancient *kapu* (taboo) system. Then drive up Lyon Hill to Fagan Memorial Cross (visible from the highway in the center of town) for the panoramic view of the entire coast. If the gate is closed, inquire at the Hotel Hana-Maui, whose lobby is across the road.

Hotel Hana-Maui serves a moderately expensive a la carte lunch, highly recommended, if only for a glimpse of life at one of the world's idyllic hideaway resorts. Other lunch options include the Hana Ranch Restaurant further up the road, or Tutu's snack shop down by the bay for burgers.

If you still have energy, head on to Hamoa Beach, 100-foot Wailua Falls, and the popular Seven Pools of ʻOheʻo Gulch in the Kipahulu section of Haleakala National Park, 12 scenic miles beyond Hana. (At this point, who's counting?) A clearly marked parking area puts you close to the ʻOheʻo Stream and its many shallow swimming pools. Below the bridge near the ocean are the most popular pools. Adventurers head up along the slippery stream bed half a mile to Makahiku Falls, and Waimoku Falls a mile beyond that. The trek can be dangerous in rainy weather; read the signs carefully and check with the ranger on duty to be sure.

The often washed-out road beyond Kipahulu is off-limits to rental cars. Turn around here and head slowly back to a good night's rest.

Umbrella-shaded tables and lounge chairs grace Hamoa Beach, once a recreation area maintained for the exclusive use of wealthy Hotel Hana Maui guests. Nestled into the verdant Hana Coast, this pearly white beach is now open to the public.

Looking like colorful single-winged butterflies fluttering through a garden of blue and white flowers, windsurfers ply the waves at world-famous Ho'okipa. The 1946 tidal wave reduced this once capacious stretch of white sand to a narrow beach faced with a rocky shelf.

The high surf and swirling currents of Ho'okipa Beach Park are a favorite playground for the world's top windsurfers. These adventurous wave riders cup the 30-knot trade winds in their mylar sails, head straight for the face of a 10 to 15-foot cresting wave.

Wai'anapanapa, one of Maui's few black-sand beaches, is the most popular feature of the Wai'anapanapa State Park just outside of Hana. A hula *halau* (dance troupe) gathers at low tide for a ceremonial invocation to the ancient gods.

The wind-tossed sugar cane fields of Pioneer Plantation stretch from the resort areas of Ka'anapali and Lahaina to the foothills and valleys of the West Maui Mountains.

The Kapalua resort is rife with golf courses, tennis clubs, luxury hotels, bed-and-breakfasts, and condominiums.

Front Street in historic Lahaina town still retains much of the charm of the old whaling days.

On the shores of Ka'anapali, a couple enjoys the fading ember of the Maui sun.

WEST MAUI

Maui's miles of sunny south and west-facing shoreline were perfect for developing a new visitor industry. These shores are sheltered from the prevailing northeast trade winds; the sun is predictable, the waters calm, the rains infrequent, the sunsets sublime; and the outlying islands—Moloka'i, Lana'i, and Kaho'olawe—give scenic depth to the horizon.

In the late 1950s, the owners of the Pioneer sugar mill chose three miles of white-sand beach at Ka'anapali, just north of Lahaina, as the place to begin West Maui's transformation into a major international resort destination. The opening of the Royal Lahaina Resort in 1962 and the Sheraton Maui Hotel a year later launched Maui's development as a visitor destination.

The West Maui tour begins beyond Ka'anapali at the far end of Honoapi'ilani Highway, where a handful of dramatic cove beaches scallop the shore. In succession southward, the coves include Honokohau Bay, Punalau, Honolua (Maui's premier winter surf spot), Slaughterhouse, and D. T. Fleming Beach Park. All but Fleming are unmarked, except for cars parked along the road. Access to the beaches is by steep paths. The water, usually rough in winter, is great in summer for snorkeling and swimming. Fleming Beach has parking, showers, and restrooms.

Past Fleming, the highway widens through the manicured Kapalua resort area. The Kapalua Bay Hotel and Villas is Maui's premier resort, a ranking assured by its turquoise-to-royal-blue water, its white-sand beaches, and its tremendous views across blustery Pailolo Channel to East Moloka'i. The exclusive Ironwoods subdivision at Oneloa Beach is home to C.E.O.s, film and music stars, and other notables. Inland, tall stands of Cook Island pines give distinctive charm to two golf courses.

Follow the main road until it becomes Lower Honoapi'ilani Road where it enters the Napili resort and residential area. The half-mile strip of low-rise hotels and condos here is flanked by gardens and serene beaches. The broad, excellent Napili Bay swimming beach is accessible by several hard-to-spot rights-of-way between the condos and hotels.

The landmark Napili Kai Beach Club, a low-rise luxury hotel at Napili Bay's northern end, is one of Hawai'i's increasingly rare "old-fashioned" hotels. Its modest design, simple interiors, and beautifully planted grounds harmonize with, rather than try to overwhelm, the environment.

The three miles between Napili and Ka'anapali are full of high-rise condo apartments and private homes. Many of West Maui's most reasonably priced beachfront rentals are at Kahana and Honokowai.

Ka'anapali was once a heavily cultivated taro-producing region, then a shipping point, and, finally, a dump for the nearby Pioneer Mill. Today, it is a world-renowned resort (*see* Beaches). Six luxury hotels and several condominiums line the beach and highway, carefully spaced to allow for gardens, pools, tennis courts, and shopping arcades.

To reach the central resort area, turn off Honoapi'ilani Highway into the second entrance, clearly marked "Ka'anapali Beach Resort." Parking for non-guests is limited, but usually available, at the Hyatt and the Westin Maui, near the Sheraton, and at Whaler's Village. By law, landowners must provide public access to the beach, but nothing was said about parking!

There is excellent snorkeling off Pu'u Keka'a (Black Rock), site of the Sheraton-Maui Hotel. The beach is the fantasyland of the Hyatt Regency Maui and Whaler's village, with great restaurants, 45 shops, and a whaling museum nearby. All along the beach is golden sand, calm water (in summer), and views across 'Au'au Channel to the gently rounded island of Lana'i.

An important part of Ka'anapali's master-planned success is its proximity to Lahaina, a real town with a real seafaring history akin to New England seaports like Nantucket and Provincetown.

Continue south on Honoapi'ilani Highway to Lahaina ("merciless sun"). Follow Front Street past the Jodo Mission (its huge Buddha and ancient palms are worth a stop) and Lahaina's shops, restaurants, and galleries. Just beyond the busy waterfront lies the heart of the old town, marked by the landmark Pioneer Inn (circa 1901), the huge banyan tree planted in 1873, and the harbor. A block further down Front Street, at the corner of Prison Street, is a public parking lot. Park the car for a one-to-two-hour walking tour.

Lahaina's history is fascinating. In prehistoric legend, an ancient king begat a daughter, Kihawahine, who on her death became a great *mo'o*, lizard-god. She apparently lived in a pit on a small island called Moku'ula, in a pond near the present

Prison Street parking lot. The pond and island were considered sacred and remained important royal sanctuaries until the mid-nineteenth century. The pond was filled in 1918 for athletic fields and a playground. (Note: Even today, respect for lizards is a basic Hawaiian emotion. The accidental deaths in door jambs of little household *geckos* are considered tragic.)

When Kamehameha the Great united the islands, he paid respect to the sacred bloodlines of Maui's chiefs

This polychromatic sea captain by artist Reems Mitchell is a relic of an era long gone. Standing on the porch of Lahaina's Pioneer Inn, the old salt surveys the harbor and silently poses for pictures with any tourist who comes his way.

by marrying two Maui princesses and establishing his royal capital at Lahaina. The foundations of his "Brick Palace," built in 1802 as the first European-style building in Hawai'i, are visible near the sea wall in front of the public library, next to the Pioneer Inn. Too hot to live in, the palace functioned as a warehouse.

The effects of the arrival of New England missionaries in the 1820s, followed by the whaling fleets, remain the most visible and celebrated chapters in the town's colorful past. For a complete recounting, read *Lahaina: Royal Capital of Hawaii* by Roy Nickerson; for a self-guided walking tour of Lahaina's 31 designated historic sites, a free booklet is available at the Pioneer Inn or at the Lahaina Restoration Foundation offices.

Returning to Honoapi'ilani Highway, head south toward Central Maui. For 15 miles the highway skirts the narrow, reef-fringed beaches of Puamana, Launiupoko, Kulanaokalai, 'Awalua, Olowalu, Ukumehame, and Papalaua. The first four beaches are popular for swimming and sunning; Puamana, Launiupoko, and Papalaua have public facilities.

As the highway climbs over the 'A'alaloloa sea cliffs to the Papawai Point scenic lookout, Molokini, Kaho'olawe, and Lana'i islands stand in full view, as well as Haleakala's southwestern coastline from Kihei and Wailea to the prominent volcanic cone, Pu'u Ola'i, at Makena.

From October to early April, the waters off Papawai Point are prime calving, nursing, and mating grounds for the humpback whales that commute each year from their Alaskan and Siberian summer feeding grounds. The whales visit all the Hawaiian Islands, but the spacious waters protected by the four islands of Maui, Moloka'i, Lana'i, and Kaho'olawe attract the largest concentration. Papawai Point lookout is the premier vantage point to watch these special visitors spouting and breaching in the sun.

Built in 1901, Lahaina's historic Pioneer Inn presides over the waterfront activities at Town Square along Wharf Street.

A safe haven for the Pacific whaling fleet, Lahaina harbor was once described as a "forest of masts." Many visitors take the charter fishing expeditions into the Pailolo Channel to wrestle and snare marlin and other pelagic fishes.

Along the white sandy stretch of Ka'anapali Beach, every day is summer. At the far right are the twin towers of the Whaler on Ka'anapali Beach resort.

Lahaina has played a major part in Island history for more than 300 years: first, as a favored recreational spot of Hawaiian royalty, then as the arena for the conflict between the raucous whalers and pious missionaries. Lahaina today is one of the world's prized playgrounds.

The new resort community of Wailea, on the southwestern side of Haleakala, boasts grand hotels, condominium clusters, and a number of championship golf courses. Developed by the Alexander & Baldwin corporation in the late 1970s and early 1980s from 10,000 acres of former Matson Navigation Company ranch land, this area is one of Hawai'i's most recent destination resort developments. The conglomeration of buildings in the distance at left is the

SOUTH MAUI

These children flash an underwater "shaka" sign (Hawaiian hand greeting) while snorkeling in Molokini Islet's lagoon.

The unique obstacles of jagged ʻaʻa lava, as here at hole #8 of the Wailea Resort's Orange Course, make sand traps seem almost pleasant.

The rich flaxen-colored hues and shimmering tangerine horizon of a south Maui sunset.

Start at Maʻalaea, south of Lahaina, where Route 31 branches from Honoapiʻilani Highway. Head southeast toward Kihei. The two-lane highway passes the long stretch of windy Maʻalaea Beach (great for expert windsurfing and long walks). Inland from the highway is the Kealia Pond bird sanctuary.

Kihei is probably the most California-influenced community in Hawaiʻi. Its boomtown atmosphere and youthful population give the area a crackling energy. Kihei offers the most affordable living on Maui. Its relatively inexpensive subdivisions and condos are home to many Canadian "snowbirds," avid fans of Kihei's no-nonsense accommodations and perfect weather. These birds show up every winter.

Six beach parks along Kihei Road provide relief from the town's condo row. The best for swimming and quiet sunning are Kamaʻole Beach Parks I, II, and III, at the south end. Most refreshing about Kihei is its sheer vitality. It's a normal town in a fabulous location. Nothing is master-planned, and almost nothing is controlled. It's exuberant and inclusive, rather than tasteful and exclusive.

South Maui is known for top-notch diving. If you are a scuba or snorkel practitioner, join a tour to Molokini Islet, a tiny, volcanic crescent about three miles off the coast. Or, if you are qualified, plunge in on your own, particularly off the rocky points of Wailea and Makena. (Your hotel activities desk will have more information.)

Farther south on Kihei Road, the condos give way to private homes on new streets. Suddenly you're in Wailea, a master-planned 1,450-acre hotel resort. The heavily irrigated landscaping is lush (in its natural state, this was a near desert), and the understated road signs remind you that this is no ordinary subdivision. Three golf courses, with homes facing the fairways, and several condominium complexes complete the tastefully framed picture. The four luxury beachfront hotels **(Stouffers, the Intercontinental, Grand Wailea, and the Four Seasons) will be joined by another, as yet unnamed, hostelry.**

Wailea's five perfect cove beaches—Keawakapu, Mokapu, Ulua (the most popular), Wailea, and Polo—are among Maui's best for swimming and snorkeling. The access routes are clearly marked on Wailea Alanui Drive, the main road through the resort.

Beyond Wailea lie some of Maui's nicest, least crowded beaches offering beautiful sunset views. Offshore is stark, low-lying Kahoʻolawe island, subject of a long-running dispute between Maui's Protect Kahoʻolawe Ohana and the U.S Navy, which was finally ordered to cease its practice bombing of Kahoʻolawe late in 1990.

South on Wailea Alanui Drive, past the hotels, is old Makena Road and several small, undeveloped but extremely worthwhile beaches. (The Beaches chapter has directions for driving to them.) Palauea Beach is the best—a flat, wide, and completely undeveloped crescent of sand just south of Polo Beach.

The road continues through the *kiawe* thicket to Poʻolenalena Beach Park, a small, sandy cove with parking, and then to the charming beachfront Keawalai Congregational Church, built of coral lime in 1832. From the shady churchyard with its turn-of-the-century gravestones, the view of the little rock-framed cove is exquisite.

Returning from the churchyard, go *mauka* to Wailea Alanui Drive. Follow the drive south, past the entrance to the Maui Prince Hotel, the most recent of Maui's lavish golf resorts. Just beyond the hotel the road turns bumpy and narrow. On your right, watch for Puʻu ʻOlaʻi volcanic cone, the area's principal landmark. Two dirt roads lead to the right, the second to Oneloa Beach, better known as Makena or Big Beach, Maui's outstanding undeveloped beach. A small cove on the ocean side of Puʻu ʻOlaʻi, Oneuli or Little Beach, is the island's most popular clothing-optional beach.

Beyond the left or south end of Big Beach, a low, black-lava point reaches into the sea. This is the tip of Maui's only recent lava flow, which apparently occurred in 1790. French explorer La Perouse reported a shallow bay here in 1786. Six years later British explorer Capt. George Vancouver mapped a large, protruding lava point in the same area, separating the present Makena Beach from La Perouse Bay.

At the south end of Makena the remains of an old fishing village are worth finding and exploring—if you have sturdy shoes. The village site, Maonakala, is within the ʻAhihi-Kinaʻu Natural Area Reserve. Follow the paved road beyond Makena to where the pavement dissolves into gravel. Keep going past the sign for the reserve, where the lava field begins. A dirt road on the right leads to a path to your left as you face the ocean. The village is among the *kiawe* trees a few hundred feet away. Remnants of the old King's Trail, which used to circle the island, are visible in the lava fields.

La Perouse Bay, at the end of the road, has a string of sandy pocket beaches which are also good for snorkeling in calm weather, but be careful of *wana*—sea urchins—in the shallow waters. The road is impassable beyond the bay.

South of Kihei and around the protruding promontory of Puʻu ʻOlaʻi, is the generous expanse of sand known as Big Beach. In the background, the weathered volcanic tufts of Haleakala's southern flank slope toward the sea.

The morning sun rising above the crest of Haleakala blanches the empty beach fronting the community of Kihei.

The setting sun over Ma'alaea Bay and Kama'ole Beach near Kihei.

A cool, gentle breeze, the swish and rustle of palms, and a hammock on the beach are the makings of a perfect South Maui vacation. Cares of the world can't penetrate this kind of blissful solitude.

The lavender fields of an orchid farm, near the slopes of the West Maui Mountains, is a scene of rare beauty and economic practicality. Local flower companies provide most of the blossoms used in the Hawai'i visitor industry for leis, arrangements, tropical drinks, and hotel pillows.

Located above Wailuku town and easily accessible by auto, is history-rich ʻIao Valley. On this site, Big Island chief Kamehameha defeated the army of Maui's ruling chief Kalanikupule.

Built in 1841 by missionary Edward Bailey as a family home, this small museum is now called Hale Hoʻikeʻike.

Wailuku, the county seat of Maui, is older than Kahului and has the island's deep water port and shipping docks.

CENTRAL MAUI

About 30,000 people, one-third of Maui's total population, live in Wailuku and Kahului, the twin towns between the West Maui Mountains and Maui's north coast. Older, picturesque Wailuku, the Maui County seat, is upland near the mouth of ʻIao Valley; Kahului is a growing port and commercial town with shopping centers, service businesses, and distributor warehouses. These stolid, seemingly unremarkable middle-class communities deserve a close look. This is where real people live.

Wailuku has been important since ancient days. Keʻopuolani, Hawaiʻi's last pure-blooded sacred *aliʻi*, was born here. She was a granddaughter of Maui's warrior king, Kekaulike, wife of Kamehameha the Conqueror, and the mother of two Hawaiian kings (Liholiho and Kauikeaouli—Kamehameha II and III, respectively), and of the tragic princess Nahiʻenaʻena.

The historic heart of Wailuku lies near the old two-story Bailey House Museum, run by the Maui Historical Society. The house, built by missionaries in 1841, today offers a glimpse of missionary life, some pre-Western Hawaiian implements and artifacts, and a permanent exhibition of mid-19th-century Maui landscapes painted by the one-time owner of the house, Edward Bailey. Next door is a 1930s mansion built for the Wailuku Sugar Company's plantation manager, worth a stop for its evocative sense of Maui's plantation days. The landmark Kaʻahumanu Church, erected in 1859 on the site of an ancient *heiau*, is a short walk down Main Street from the museum.

At the corner of Main and Market, turn *makai*, toward the sea, on Market, past the funky ʻIao Theater, which now houses the Maui Community Theater, to picturesque Vineyard Street. Several small restaurants cluster there, featuring Island, American, and Asian cuisine.

ʻIao Valley State Park and the famous ʻIao Needle, Maui's most photographed natural landmark, are beyond Wailuku on Route 32. From the parking area beneath the Needle, several paved trails wind through tropical gardens to lovely ʻIao Stream. Beyond the Needle the valley ends in a great "amphitheater," with soaring cliffs, deep in the heart of the West Maui Mountains.

The mouth of the valley, near the present Kepaniwai Park and Heritage Gardens, was the scene of a fierce battle between Maui's defending army under Chief Kalanikupule and the implacable forces of Kamehameha from the Big Island, who sealed his conquest of Maui here in 1790. Kepaniwai means "dammed waters." The 'Iao Stream is said to have been literally blocked with the bodies of fallen warriors. The defeated Maui chiefs, the dowager queen Kaola, and 11-year-old princess Ke'opuolani fled into the valley and over the near-vertical cliffs to Olowalu near Lahaina, then by canoe to the island of Moloka'i.

Outside Wailuku on Highway 30 is the Maui Tropical Plantation at Waikapu, a popular visitor attraction. Its 120 acres showcase the variety of Hawai'i's crops, fruits, flowers, and exotics. Indoor exhibits explain the history, economics, and uses of Hawai'i's most famous agricultural exports.

Kanaha Beach Park near the Kahului airport is the area's busiest beach. When the trade winds are "up," this long and shady beach swarms with an international mob of windsurfers. Otherwise, it's quiet.

Old Wailuku retains its unique 1890s flavor with its storefront facades and wood plank sidewalks. Life is still a beat slower here, keeping time a bit out of step.

The famed Ho'okipa Beach Park and surfing area near the small community of Pa'ia is also known as Ho'okipa Lefts and Rights, describing the direction of waves.

Wailuku town looks as if it is spilling from the mouth of 'Iao Valley in the West Maui Mountains. Light-green patches of sugar cane flank its left side, while on the right the uniform rows of a macadamia nut orchard span the foothills.

On Highway 30, on the way to Kihei, Wailea, Lahaina, and Ka'anapali, is the Tropical Plantation. Visitors are invited into 120 acres of lush fields to see a variety of Hawai'i's famous crops, fruits, flowers, and exotics close up.

This delicate white hibiscus, koki'o Ke'oke'o, among the most ornamental of Hawai'i's native species, grows wild between 1,000 and 3,000 feet above sea level.

On the west side of High Street, in Wailuku's Historic District, is Maui's earliest existing Christian church. Built in 1837, the white-painted wood and plastered stone Ka'ahumanu Church once held Hawaiian language services for a primarily Hawaiian congregation.

"King Sugar" began its reign over Island industry in the 1860s, when America's Civil War blockades cut off Southern sugar from world markets. Pictured here is the Pu'unene Sugar Mill, still a functioning plantation.

The white-sand crescent of Hamoa Beach is a unique sight along the lava-rough Hana Coast. The origin of the name "Hamoa" is not certain—it is believed to be a shortened version of Haʻamoa, which is an old name for Samoa. Access to the beach is on private property owned by the Hana Ranch Company, and since the 1930s Hamoa has been used soley by wealthy guests of the Hotel Hana Maui. Recently the general public was given access to the swimming area. Unprotected from the open sea, the surf off this 1,000-foot-long beach was a favorite surfing spot in ancient times and is listed as a "must surf" area when visiting Maui.

M A U I
B E A C H E S

Maui's 120-mile coastline includes 32 miles of first-class beachfront. The longest stretches are on the western shores—18 miles of sand and calm water from Olowalu past Lahaina to Kapalua, and almost continuously from Ma'alaea through Kihei to Wailea near the southwestern corner of the island. In addition, coves with lovely beaches nestle among the cliffs and lava outcroppings at the island's extremities: north of Kapalua, at Hana, and south of Wailea. The north-shore beaches are smaller and less inviting for visitors because of pounding surf and stiff winds, which create unending erosion problems. Twenty-four state and county beach parks dot Maui's shoreline. Few have lifeguards, but most have restrooms, freshwater showers, and parking.

Maui has at least one beach to satisfy every taste. Surfers gravitate to Ho'okipa, Ma'alaea, Honolua, and Lahaina. Bodysurfers head for Slaughterhouse, Makena, Hamoa, and Baldwin Beach. Windsurfers call Maui mecca, and Ho'okipa, Ma'alaea, and Kanaha are its top shrines. Sunbathers have their secret coves or they simply step out of their hotels, which are situated on a vast majority of Maui's most placid swimming and sunning beaches. When the sea is calm, snorkelers have an unmatched selection of sand-and-rocky-point configurations, particularly at Wailea and Makena in South Maui, Pu'u Keka'a at Ka'anapali, and at Kapalua, Honolua, and Fleming beaches near Kapalua.

A "menu" of Maui's best-known, best-loved and best-kept-secret beaches follows. By all means, spend a complete day at one of them, preferably facing west to the sunset. Take plenty of food and water, a beach umbrella, heavy-duty sunscreen, swim fins and snorkel, a book or two, a long-sleeve shirt, and long pants. (Right after sunset you'll feel chilly.)

Note: All beaches in Hawai'i are public up to the vegetation line above the high-water mark. Rights-of-way to the beach from public roads are marked (some better than others), even in exclusive beachfront residential areas and resorts.

Makena Beach aka Big Beach aka Oneloa Beach

Whichever name it goes by, this isolated, end-of-the-road spot is Maui's favorite. The water is clear, the views are wide-open. There is no sign of civilization anywhere, and the "shore-break" waves usually range between frisky and challenging. Makena Beach gained fame in the late 1960s as a back-to-nature colony. Sanitation and other problems finally forced police and health officials to close it down. The only reminder of those days is Little Beach, a sandy cove reached by a short trail from the end of Big Beach, where free spirits continue to sunbathe in the buff. Snorkeling off the rocky points at Makena and Little Beach is fantastic. Almost any time between November and March, a few feet beneath the surface might be heard the faint, high-pitched clicks, moans, and whistles of the humpback whales, whose "songs" travel for miles underwater.

HOʻOKIPA BEACH PARK
Right alongside the Hana Highway beyond Paʻia, Hoʻokipa is the best-known surfing and windsurfing beach on Maui. Big winter surf rolls into the shallow bay and breaks across the beachfront, not a hundred yards offshore. Big-wave windsurfing was virtually invented here. Windsurfers and board surfers now divide the waves (windsurfers to the left; board surfers to the right). Spectators get a double thrill watching surfers and their wind-borne counterparts on the same waves.

KAIHALULU BEACH

In calm sea conditions, this hidden gem of a beach on the far side of Ka'uiki Hill in Hana has some of the best, most intimate snorkeling in the state. It's like swimming in an aquarium. Carved from the volcanic cinder cone that created Ka'uiki Hill, Kaihalulu cove is often called Red Sand Beach. The blue water lapping against the reddish sand is stunningly beautiful. Although the small beach is protected from direct sea action by a jagged lava barrier, swimmers should still exercise caution.

KA'ANAPALI BEACH

Maui's resort beach *par excellence*, Ka'anapali is a broad, three-mile expanse of golden sand, inviting water, and terrific people-watching. There's little solitude here. Ka'anapali is for social beach-going, seeing, and being seen. The busiest part fronts the lively restaurants at Whaler's Village between the Ka'anapali Beach Hotel and the Westin Maui. During the day, a sand volleyball court draws the deeply tanned muscle crowd and the thickest concentration of singles. As the sun sinks in a blaze of color behind a distant island, and music drifts out to the beach, couples play out their dreams of a cocktail and a barefoot walk in the sand.

Hoby-cat sailing is one of the many activities offered at the Ka'anapali resort complex. Experienced instructors teach novice sailors in the placid waters of the Pailolo Channel between the islands of Maui and Moloka'i.

The gentle humpback whales, once hunted off the coast of Lahaina, now migrate from the North Pacific to the warm waters of Hawai'i to calve their young. Small boats conduct whale-watching tours from Lahaina, Ma'alaea, and Kihei to develope awareness and educate visitors about the life and behavior of these seagoing mammals. *photo by Mike Nolan*

M A U I
ADVENTURES

If your vacation requires more than a memorable tan, Maui offers snorkeling off your hotel beach, deep-sea fishing, windsurfing, sailing, kayaking, hiking, bicycling down Haleakala, horseback riding, scuba diving on Molokini, or cruising to Lana'i.

Maui's calm leeward ocean, enclosed by four islands, provides the most scenic, hospitable, and comfortable sailing water in the state. From November to April these same waters are the winter home of the North Pacific's humpback whales. A wide variety of charter boats are available for whale-watching, sailing, diving, fishing, and sightseeing. Other craft, large and small, offer sunset dinner cruises. Most commercial boating operations are based at Lahaina and Ma'alaea harbors, close to West Maui resorts.

High-energy wind and sea conditions, plus year-round warm weather, make Maui a natural for the athletically inclined. The island has become one of the world's great water-sports capitals, with international surfing contests, long-distance swimming meets, offshore fishing tournaments, inter-island canoe and kayak races, windsurfing competitions, and inter-island and trans-Pacific yacht races. On shore, brawny "triathletes," daring hang-glider pilots, and mud-stained hikers carry the "just do it" ethos to new extremes. International golf and tennis tournaments proliferate, and the Maui invitational basketball tournament draws athletes from colleges across the United States.

On Maui, there is energy everywhere—in the big mid-Pacific water, in the stiff trade winds, and on this young volcanic island itself. Everything converges with spectacular power and astonishing gentleness. You can *feel* the vibrant energy as soon as you arrive.

NOTE: *KAPU* (taboo, beware, avoid)

The recent proliferation of "thrill craft"—jetskis, parasail rides, speedboats, dune buggies, and other devices that have no transportation purpose but in which the mechanical ride itself is the "thrill"—has generated alarm and resentment in Hawai'i. As a visitor, you should be aware of how intrusive the noise, air pollution, danger, and general blight from these activities are to other users of Hawai'i's waters, forests, and mountains.

Their threat to endangered sea and plant life makes them the subject of very serious concern among not only local environmentalists, but others who wish to defend Hawai'i's natural spirit and integrity. This attitude is called *aloha 'aina*, love for the land. We hope you will respect and share it.

This intreped para-sailing human kite dangles from a colorful parachute above the inter-island cruise ship, the *Ocean Independence*.

The man holding this puffer fish released it soon after the photo was taken.

Powerful ocean currents and the blustering of trade winds have made the once unknown Ho'okipa Beach a mecca for windsurfers.

WHALE-WATCHING

Whale-watching is Maui's premier seasonal attraction. The island-protected leeward waters are a natural amphitheater for the migratory North Pacific humpback whales that leave coastal Alaska in the fall and arrive in November.

During their stay until April to calve and mate, the whales eat little (living off their blubber for six months). But they do sing. To hear them is one of Maui's unique experiences. Simply swim into some open, calm water at least 10 feet deep anywhere along Maui's southwestern shores during the winter. Take a deep breath and sink a foot or two beneath the surface, holding perfectly still. If any whales are around, you'll hear high-pitched whistles, low moans and clicking sounds—40-ton intelligent mammals communicating with each other, a mile to maybe five miles away.

A rainbow floats over Polipoli, located in the Mākena area on Maui's South Coast. This park is a favorite local recreation spot with its hiking trails, freshwater spring, cabin, and campground.

Whales usually can be spotted by the plumes of mist or "spouts" they shoot into the air as they exhale. Occasionally a humpback will repeatedly jump almost clear of the water. This "breaching" is tremendously exciting to watch. If you go on a whale-watching charter or simply watch from shore, be sure to take binoculars and a good telephoto lens for your camera.

Federal and State regulations protect the endangered humpbacks from harassment. All boats, except bona fide research vessels, must maintain a minimum distance of 100 yards.

During whale season, Lahaina and Ma'alaea harbors are filled with sailboats, catamarans, fishing craft, and big excursion boats offering chances to view the whales in well-provisioned comfort. Sightings cannot be guaranteed, but are frequent enough to keep the mini-industry flourishing. Excursions usually last about four hours and may include a light breakfast, lunch, or sunset dinner. There are several ocean sports operations that offer excursions out of Ma'alaea and Lahaina. A number of sleek 36-foot catamarans and a few sailing yachts take groups out over the "whale roads." Prices vary, depending on the length of the sail and food service. Private charters are available by advance reservation.

ON FOOT

The best hiking and walking on Maui are either at the summit or on the broad, lower slopes of Haleakalā.

Two mildly demanding options are worth special notice. One is through Polipoli State Park's highland forests. The other is into Haleakalā's surreal, lunar-like summit crater. Several other short hikes are listed in the "Tours" section of this volume. Note particularly one along the Hana coast at Wai'ānapanapa State Park and another at the waterfalls to 'Ohe'o Gulch in Kipahulu.

Polipoli State Park, a remote forest sanctuary high above the gardens of Kula at the 6,200-foot level on Haleakalā, is one of Maui's least-visited parks. The latter half of the 10-mile road into the park is unpaved and often severely rutted. Four-wheel-drive vehicles are recommended, although in good weather regular cars usually can make it.

Polipoli has a unique mixture of native and introduced plant species. Redwoods planted at the turn of the century, cypress groves, stands of eucalyptus, cryptomeria pines, and *Acacia koa* predominate. Fog and clouds regularly cloak the high trees and muffle the cries of pheasant and grouse. In addition to game birds, the feral pigs and wild goats make this area popular with hunters. This is one place where Hawai'i doesn't look anything like what you expected.

The entrance to the park is marked. The trails are well signed, including mileage information for day hikes (the Redwood Trail is recommended). Seasonal pig and bird hunting requires a license. An overnight cabin with a cook stove and bunks for ten is available. To reserve space call the State Parks office in Wailuku. Polipoli State Park is reached via Route 377, past the Kula Botanical Garden to a left turn on Waipoli Road.

Haleakalā. Thirty-four miles of hiking trails crisscross Haleakalā National Park, but most of them are for overnighters. Day-trippers are pretty well restricted to leaving from and returning to either of two places. Sliding Sands Trail starts at the visitor center at the summit, the Halemau'u Trail from the parking lot at the 8,000-foot level on the road to the summit. For information on weather and mileage, check in at park headquarters or at the summit visitor center.

The Sliding Sands Trail descends to the crater floor's multi-hued cinder cones. Distances are deceiving

The Waiʻānapanapa trail, along the Hana coast, is blanketed with *hala* leaves. Ferns, ti plants, and a variety of trees shade the tranquil setting as crashing waves boom onto nearby Waiʻānapanapa Beach.

Sailing off the coast of Kaʻanapali—past Whaler's Village, and The Whaler on Kaʻanapali Beach resorts—is an excellent way to experience the deep blue waters of the Pailolo Channel and see the vivid panorama of the resorts' waterfront.

Each year thousands of visitors drive to the 10,023-foot summit of Haleakalā in the predawn hours to witness the sunrise. Other more adventurous souls remain to hike the austere environs. The crater, an erosion of volcanic material, measures 21 miles in circumference, 3,000 feet deep, and 19 square miles in diameter.

in this otherworldly landscape. What looks like a quick jaunt is often an hours-long journey. To reach the floor and return to the rim requires a full day, so turn back *before* your energy runs out. The uphill, high-altitude return climb on this "sliding" trail can be exhausting. Be sure to pack water for this trip.

The Halemau'u trail to Hōlua Cabin is an eight-mile, six-hour roundtrip. The first mile descends from the parking lot through alpine scrubland to the rim, then the trail descends in a series of dramatic switchbacks and across a meadow to the cabin. The views of Haleakalā's northern flanks, the lava rivers of cloud-wrapped Ko'olau Gap, and the moist cliffs of Leleiwi are the prime rewards of this popular hike.

Overnight hikes into the corners of Haleakalā's vast summit crater require careful planning, adequate camping gear, rainwear, food, and water. The Kapalaoa, Palikū, and Hōlua overnight cabins and campsites at Palikū and Hōlua are the focuses of overnight trips. The cabins should be reserved three months in advance by writing Haleakalā National Park. Cabins campers must register at park headquarters before setting out.

Tour boat companies from the ports of Ma'alaea and Kihei shuttle snorkelers and scuba divers to the underwater reserve around Molokini Islet. Visitors of all ages participate in expeditions to explore the reefs surrounding this crescent-shaped volcanic crater.

BICYCLING DOWN HALEAKALĀ

Bob Kiger, a retired Hollywood ad man, on his birthday in 1983 took his bike to the 10,000-foot summit of Haleakalā so he could coast down 38 twisting miles to the seashore town of Pa'ia. Inspired by his experience, he bought a few mountain bikes, developed special "megabrakes," and opened a business. Today several companies offer the spectacular trip in small escorted groups on special mountain bikes with very fancy brakes, helmets, rain gear, hearty breakfasts, picnic lunches, guides, escort vans, hotel pick-up service, and lots of insurance. The six-hour descent is carefree, the pace is reasonable, and the scenery dizzyingly beautiful. The commercial operators require strict adherence to a 20-mph speed limit, permit no passing once in line, and require frequent stops to let cars pass. Children must be big enough to straddle a 26-inch cruiser bike; those under 16 require a parental release.

Most of the bike-ride operations offer trips at sunrise, midday, and sunset, and bad-weather insurance. The cost may seem as steep as the mountain, but it's a bargain for such a once-in-a-lifetime thrill.

SNORKELING

Of all Hawai'i's islands, Maui is the best for novice snorkelers. The coves north of Ka'anapali and south of Kihei, characterized by sand bottoms between low lava "arms" or points, are perfect for easy snorkeling. Getting into the water via the beach and swimming to the points is easy. The underwater rocks, reefs, and coral are ideal for watching butterflyfish, tangs, Moorish idols, wrasse, surgeonfish, *manini*, the famous *humuhumunukunukuapua'a* (state fish of Hawai'i), ulua, parrotfish, green sea turtles, moray eels, spiny lobsters, sea shrimp, *wana* (sea urchins—don't touch!), and colorful coral colonies.

The very best beaches for snorkeling are at Mākena and Wailea, at Kamaole Beach Parks II and III in Kihei, Olowalu, and Pu'u Keka'a (Black Rock) at Ka'anapali Beach. Kapalua, Slaughterhouse Beach, and Honolua, at the northern end of the West Maui coastline, are excellent during placid summer weather. In winter, these exposed areas are frequently rough, dangerous, and no fun for a novice.

The most popular offshore snorkeling is at Molokini Islet, a small volcanic crescent about three miles off the Mākena shore. Every morning a fleet of commercial tour boats heads for the island's little bay for a few hours of snorkeling and an early lunch. Thousands of reef fish tamed by regular feedings literally eat bread out of your hand—environmentally questionable, perhaps, but great for photography. Most operators rent underwater cameras.

As Molokini's popularity and crowds have increased, some commercial snorkeling tours have opted for Hulopo'e Bay Marine Preserve and other secluded coves on the island of Lana'i. A number of ocean activities businesses, operating out of Lahaina and Kihei offer a range of daily group excursions to Molokini and Lana'i from Ma'alaea Harbor. You'll receive snorkeling equipment, breakfast, lunch, and some lively demonstrations of sea life.

The constant bluster of the trade winds and the force of open ocean waves that pile on the submerged rocky shelf combine to make the best spot for windsurfing in the world.

The protected waters of the Auʻau channel between the islands of Maui and Lanaʻi make the perfect venue for local competitive canoe club beam-reach practice runs.

Decending the 10,000-foot Haleakalā summit to sea level without pedaling may not be the perfect activity for everyone, but this ultimate bike ride is certainly a rush you'll never forget.

A school of Milletseed Butterflyfish (*lau-wiliwili*) rally around some lucky snorkelers. In 1977, the Molokini Shoal Marine Life Conservation District was established to protect the waters off the islet from illegal fishing and overuse by the snorkel and dive tour companies.

Honolua Bay used to be a secret spot for locals only. The tubular rights of the strong north swells in winter make this one of the best high-performance breaks on the island.

This sperm whale skeleton on display at Whaler's Village in Ka'anapali was erected to commemorate the area's history and to remind all who live and visit here of our connection to the mammals of the sea.

An 'ipu, Hawaiian percussion instrument used to accompany kahiko (ancient) hula and chant, is made from a hollowed and polished bottle gourd. The chanter thumps different parts of the rounded bottom and neck to vary the pitch of the drumming.

Planet Hollywood, the movie stars' answer to the Hard Rock Cafe, opened its Lahaina shop in 1995 in an old Front Street building.

Maui boasts some of the finest restaurants in the world, offering every type of cuisine from Nouvelle to Oriental, Western to Italian.

MAUI
CIVILIZATION

Bartenders will shake, blend, or stir any concoction your imagination can create.

Hali'imaili General Store and Cafe in Upcountry Maui near the town of Makawao has an inventive menu and art-covered walls.

Aloha Cantina, one of Lahaina's more interesting eateries, offers a Mexican menu of tacos and burritos, tostadas and margaritas.

There are two ways to spend your time and money on Maui: staying close to the resorts or mingling with the local residents. The Kapalua, Ka'anapali, and Wailea master-planned resorts include excellent shops and galleries, posh restaurants, carefully crafted pools, and romantic bars. But forty minutes beyond the resort gates, there are smaller and less expensive restaurants, shops and watering places that offer some down-to-earth alternatives.

In Wailuku's spirited bars and Upcountry Maui's cozy lodges, "locals" and visitors mix freely. From Kahului's general-purpose shopping to Makawao's casually chic dining and Pa'ia's artsy-craftsy browsing, you'll find there is much more to Maui than pricey lobster tails and logo-covered beach towels.

SHOPPING

At the high end are the **Kapalua Shops** at Kapalua, **Whalers' Village** at Ka'anapali and **Wailea Shopping Village** at Wailea—collections of resort shops for top-drawer browsing and buying. Although more plebian, **Lahaina** can also be a fabulous place for shopping. Countless **Front Street** vendors sell silly t-shirts, beachwear, scrimshaw jewelry, knickknacks, bric-a-brac, whirligig hats, and other cleverly useless items. For inexpensive gifts to take home for a few laughs, these shops can't be beat. And Front Street is like a carnival for people-watching—there's even a tattoo shop. Lahaina's most interesting mini-malls include **505 Front Street**, the **Wharf**, **844 Front Street**, and the **Cannery**.

On the opposite side of the island, **Kahului** has the best general shopping. Along Ka'ahumanu Avenue and geared to the local market are the **Ka'ahumanu Shopping Center** (the biggest, with Sears and Liberty House, Hawai'i's leading department store), **Maui Mall**, and **Kahului Shopping Center**. Prices here are lower than in the resort areas, so Kahului is your best bet for standard beachgear, books, food for your condo, maybe clothes.

Specialty shops are worth seeking out, and they are all over the island. Indeed, Maui is a mecca for artists and craftsmen, and you will find in their shops everything from hand-painted silks to woven baskets, Hawaiian quilts, books, musical instruments, recorded music, handmade clothes to surfing equipment and beachwear, astonishing original collectibles made from fibers, woods, clays, and glass. In

Makawao you'll even find a Western general store-style outfitter for the area's real cowboys.

Art Galleries

Maui's thriving art scene is a study in contrasts. Along Lahaina's Front Street, Red Skelton's clown paintings, "Dali" prints, and hundreds of dolphin interpretations share window space with sublime landscapes and sensuous flower studies. By all the evidence, Maui's art market is booming, but sometimes it's hard to figure out how much is actually art and how much is just market.

The theme of much of Maui's commercial art is the underwater environment featuring whales, dolphins, reef fish, and lots of blue paint. The international success of **Robert Wyland**, whose huge, inspiring whale murals can be seen around the world, as well as the immense popularity of **Robert Lyn Nelson's** work, has spawned a Maui school of marine art whose headquarters is Maui, whale-watching capital of the world. Wyland/Nelson imitators are plentiful and it's fascinating to tour the galleries, most of them along Front Street, just to see their work.

Among Maui's better artists are **Curtis Wilson Cost, Pamela Andelin, George Allan, Eddie Flotte, Margaret Bedell,** and **Ian Tremewen.** You can find these and other talented painters at galleries all over the island.

Local Events

For data on local music and cultural events, fairs, community lu'au, and special celebrations, see the daily *Maui News* "Datebook" and "Calendar of Events" columns. Look for a community fundraising lu'au if you want the real flavor and spirit of Hawaiian feasting.

West Maui's artist community has flourished and the number of galleries in the area has doubled.